Easy Guitar Chord & Lead Tricks

by Jonathan Kehew

Acknowledgments..2

Introduction...2

PART 1: *First-Position Chord Tricks*.................3

The D–C–G Trick..3

The Universal Riff Trick 5

The Em7 Trick 7

The E–G–A, One-Finger Blues Trick 9

PART 2: *Up-The-Neck Chord Tricks* 10

The E–A Trick 10

The B Trick 12

The Power-Chord Scale Trick 14

The One-Finger, Major–Minor Trick 17

The A–D Trick 19

The Fmaj7 Trick 21

The E Major Trick 23

The Open-String Blues Trick 24

The Only Two-Chord Blues Trick 25

The Power Chord–Open String Trick 27

The Pinky Sixth Trick 29

The Melodic Shuffle Trick 31

The Chord Play Trick 33

PART 3: *Lead Guitar Tricks*.............................35

The Double Stop Trick 35

The Box 1 Trick 37

The Box 1–Box 2 Trick 39

The Sixth Trick 41

The Turnaround–Intro Trick 43

The Dorian Mode Trick 45

The Mixolydian Mode Trick 47

To access video visit:
www.halleonard.com/mylibrary

Enter Code
8373-8387-5379-4851

ISBN 978-1-7051-0293-0

Visit Hal Leonard Online at
www.halleonard.com

Contact us:
Hal Leonard
7777 West Bluemound Road
Milwaukee, WI 53213
Email: info@halleonard.com

In Europe, contact:
Hal Leonard Europe Limited
42 Wigmore Street
Marylebone, London, W1U 2RN
Email: info@halleonardeurope.com

In Australia, contact:
Hal Leonard Australia Pty. Ltd.
4 Lentara Court
Cheltenham, Victoria, 3192 Australia
Email: info@halleonard.com.au

Acknowledgments

This book is dedicated with deep love and thanks to my family for their support!

Thanks also to Jim Craig of Hogeye Music, Evanston, Illinois and Paul Neri of Connecticut for keeping my instruments running so well. I highly recommend Paul's book, *The Acoustic Guitar Repair Detective*, published by Hal Leonard.

Introduction

A musician makes music appear out of thin air, and like any good magician, we each have our secret skills. Welcome to my collection of tricks! None of these are very difficult—they are *accessible*, I like to say. As with any sleight-of-hand tricks, they need polishing before they can become part of your act.

As you master these tricks, you will probably recognize some familiar riffs, intros, and songs. I hope this book motivates you to get creative with these tricks and make them your own.

Enjoy and happy practicing!

PART 1
First-Position Chord Tricks

The D–C–G Trick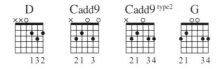

This particular sequence and unique chord voicing combination has spawned a lot of famous songs.

The D itself is your standard, first-position D major chord. The chord that comes next is a beauty: the Cadd9 chord. Note the third finger should remain on the B string, third fret when changing from D to Cadd9. In fact, it remains in place as you change to the four-finger G chord as well!

You've given you two types of the Cadd9. For the examples below, we'll stick with the first type. If you've never played the four-finger G before, note the unique chiming sound you get on the treble strings. Here's the first example in standard notation and tablature, showing you each chord that will be used:

EXAMPLE 1

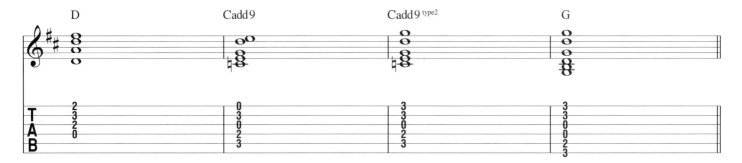

You could write a book on all the creative (and famous) ways this exact chord sequence can be embellished upon. What you see here is just the tip of the iceberg!

Example 2 features a boom-boom-chick rhythm kicked off by the root note of the chord. Note the fun *bass note run* that sends you back to the D chord!

EXAMPLE 2

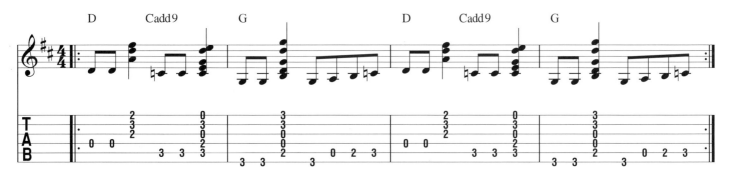

Example 3 includes hammer-ons with the boom-chick feel. I recommend *alternate picking* (down–up) when playing the eighth-note run at the end.

EXAMPLE 3

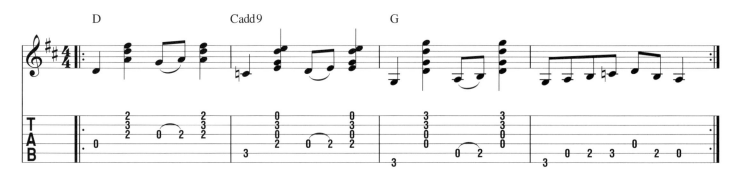

Example 4 can be played with a pick or with bare fingers using a thumb–index–thumb–middle combination. Use alternate picking when playing this one with a pick.

EXAMPLE 4

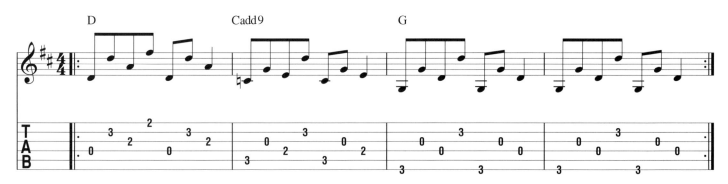

The Universal Riff Trick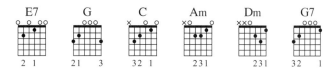

This riff represents the first time I ever added a melodic fill to my chord strumming. I was on top of the world! In time, I realized that this riff connected melodically with any open-position chord I could think of. Now *that's* a keeper!

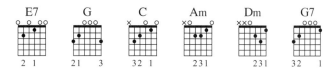

The "universality" can be traced back to the source of the Universal Riff: the E minor/G major pentatonic scale. Memorize this scale—you'll find yourself drawing on it endlessly, way beyond the trick presented here. There is no scale more useful!

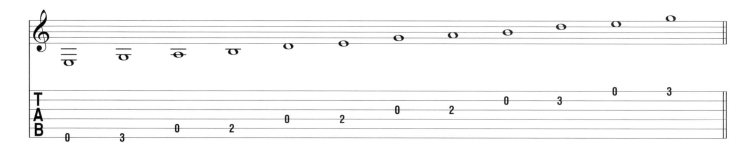

In Example 1, we link the Universal Riff to an E7 to establish a classic blues groove.

EXAMPLE 1

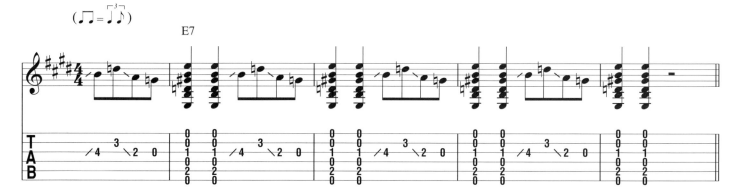

Example 2 changes to the key of G major for a country sound.

EXAMPLE 2

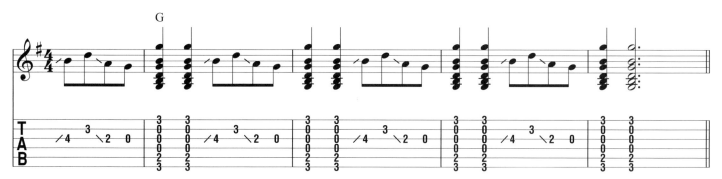

Example 3 navigates us through the timeless I–vi–ii–V7 chord progression with our Universal Riff fearlessly guiding the way!

EXAMPLE 3

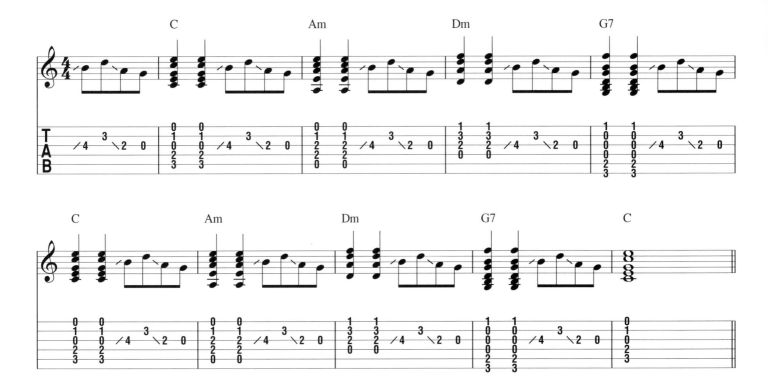

The Em7 Trick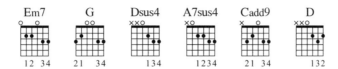

This four-finger E minor chord is actually an Em7, thanks to the third finger on the B string, third fret. This trick relies on maintaining the third and fourth fingers exactly where they are—don't lift them off for any reason! And the other chords will incorporate them even as the bass notes change. Here are the chords we'll use in the following exercises:

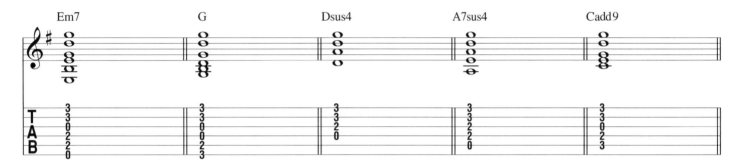

The first example shows the chords in standard notation and tablature.

EXAMPLE 1

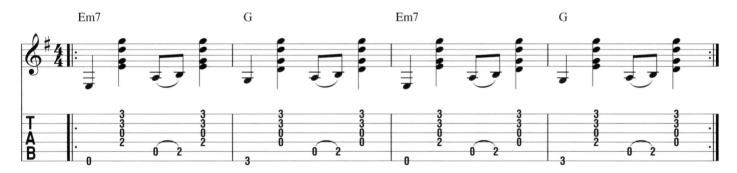

Example 2 features Em7's best friend: the four-finger G. The hammer-on keeps things chugging right along; these hammer-ons between chord strums reflect an invaluable skill that can sound like two guitarists playing at once!

EXAMPLE 2

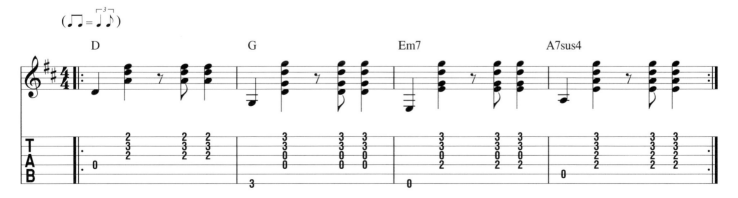

Example 3 is in the key of D, but that doesn't stop the Em7 Trick! The A7sus4 adds yet another chord to the family.

EXAMPLE 3

Example 4 reverses the order so that the four-finger G comes first. How about that Cadd9? At this point, you should have serious grooves in the tips of your third and fourth fingers! Note the subtle change from Dsus4 to D at the end—it keeps things interesting.

EXAMPLE 4

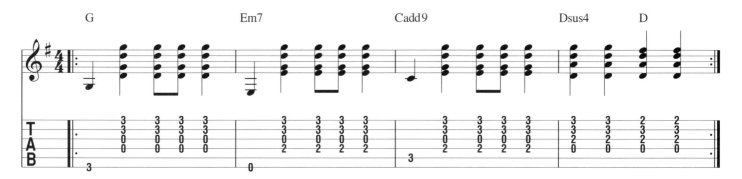

The E-G-A, One-Finger Blues Trick ▶

Sometimes, great sounds are very easily accomplished with a single, simple technique. One finger can equal lots of blues power!

This trick takes advantage of the natural G major chord hiding in plain sight: the open B, G, and D strings. Combine it with the one-finger E5 power chord and the one-finger A5 or A major chords, and the licks write themselves! Here are the chords we'll use for the following examples:

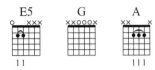

Example 1 is as powerful as it is easy. Remember to really lean into that pull-off from A to G. Don't worry if the resulting G is a little quiet. Just hustle back to the E, and keep on strumming!

EXAMPLE 1

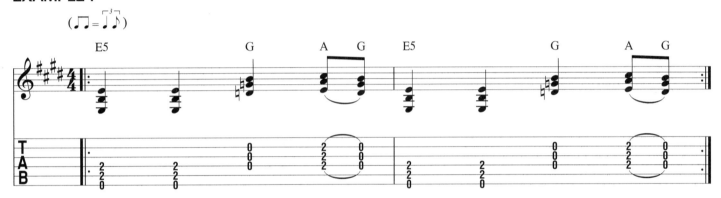

Examples 2 and 3 are easy variations on Example 1. This trick has a lot of possibilities. Learn them, and then compose your own!

EXAMPLE 2

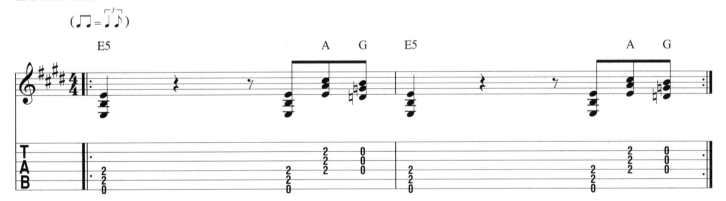

EXAMPLE 3

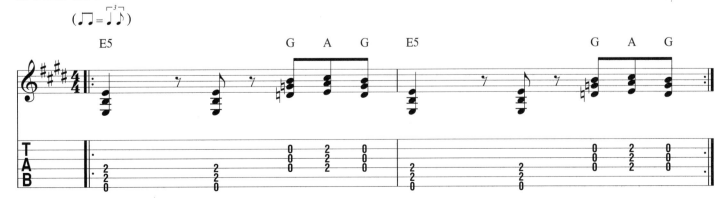

PART 2
Up-The-Neck Chord Tricks

The E–A Trick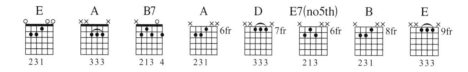

Let's start with our good friend, the E major chord. After a strum or two, relax your third finger across the second fret. The goal is to achieve clear sounds on the second, third, and fourth strings. Keep your thumb aimed up at the ceiling to help with the pressure you'll need. Be precise with your pick, and you'll have an instant A major chord. Here are the chords we'll use for the following examples:

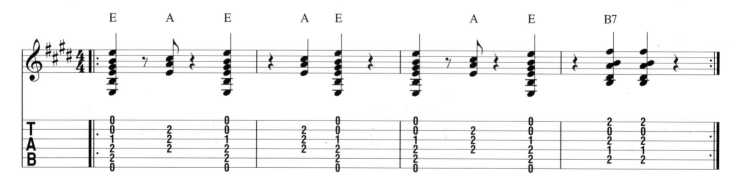

Rocking back and forth between this A and E is a trick with a *ton* of practical applications, and an easy B7 is waiting nearby to complete our trio of I–IV–V chords. But that's just for starters! In this first example, here is each chord shape, progressing from one to the next in standard notation and tablature:

EXAMPLE 1

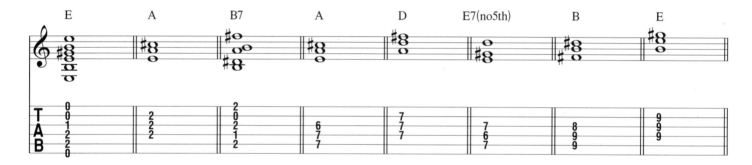

You can move this riff up the neck—just limit your picking to the strings you fret and avoid picking the open strings. You now have the classic I–IV chord progression in any key you please!

Example 2 creates a classic early rock 'n' roll groove. You've heard this one a million times! The B7 at the end "ties a bow" on the riff.

EXAMPLE 2

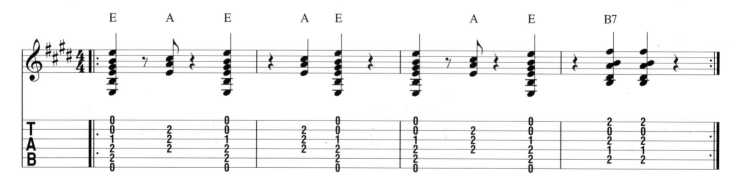

Example 3 moves the riff up the neck to the key of A. And the E7(no5th) does a handy job of implying the V chord. It's all we need!

EXAMPLE 3

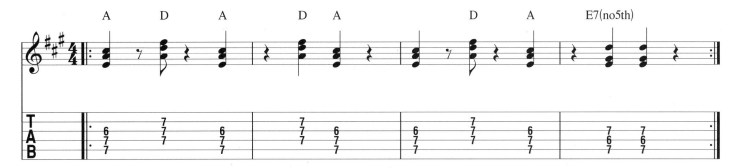

Example 4 walks us up and down the neck using the E–A Trick. Whether we are on the I chord, the IV, or the V, our trick is waiting for us!

EXAMPLE 4

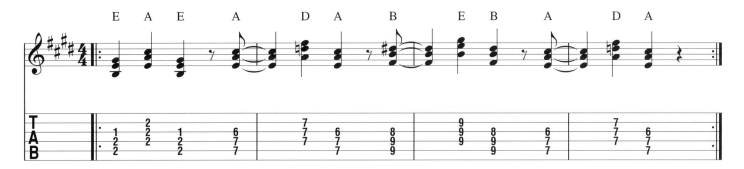

The B Trick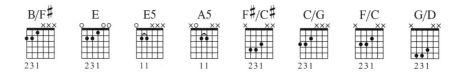

Many students have asked me, "Where's the B major chord?" The B Trick guides you right to it, and a whole lot of new possibilities open up!

The B major chord has been waiting for you all this time, right next to E major. Strum only the three bass strings and you're done. Relax your fretting hand fingers to dampen the three treble strings to avoid any unwanted "harmony." Here is the first example, showing you the chords we'll use for the other examples:

EXAMPLE 1

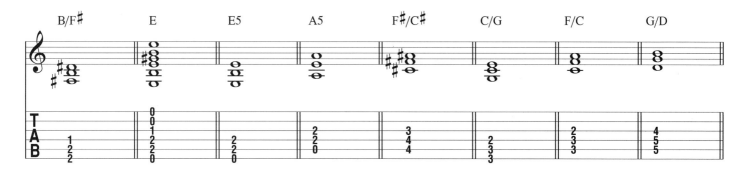

And here are the chords shown in standard notation and tablature:

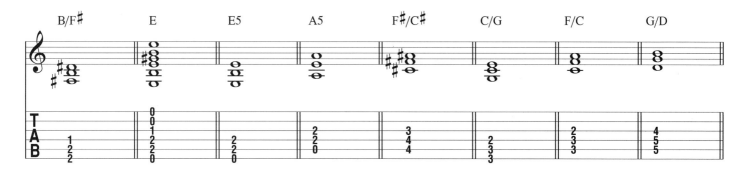

The chord progressions here give you several options to get you started. By the way, we are sticking with three-note voicings for all of the chords to match the tight, punchy sound of our new B. Don't be freaked out by these *slash chords*. B/F♯ just indicates that our B chord has F♯ as the lowest note. Chords like this one are known as *inverted chords*. There's nothing to "fret" about!

Example 2 is in the key of E, so you can use our new B chord to substitute for our old standby B7. Easy!

EXAMPLE 2

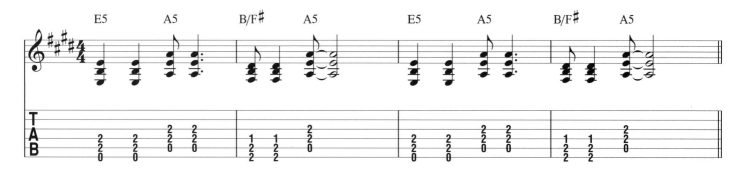

In Example 3 on the next page, slide your E major grip up two frets to arrive at the V chord, F♯ major. Aim your pick well, and watch out for unwanted noise from the open strings.

EXAMPLE 3

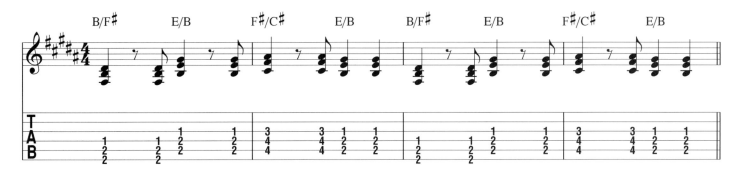

Example 4 moves Example 3 into the key of C. Now go ahead and move this riff up the neck!

EXAMPLE 4

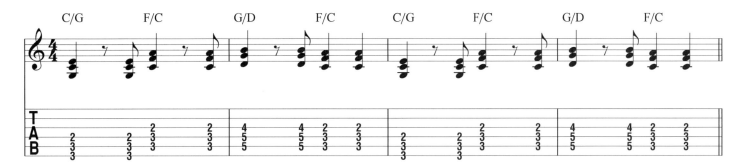

The Power-Chord Scale Trick

Ah, the humble power chord. Did you know there are tons of melodic riffs waiting for you, orbiting around this classic grip? Here's the C5 power chord to get started:

We'll use the C5 power chord and the C major scale to illustrate this trick. Here, you'll melodically combine a single power chord with different scale degrees (and altered ones too).

First, get warmed up on the C major scale. We'll be using many (but not all) of these notes. A few of the following exercises include a raised or lowered scale degree. Make a note of the musical effect this has!

EXAMPLE 1

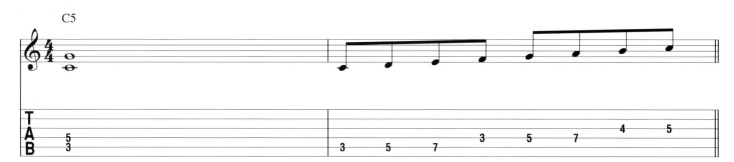

Each one of the riffs here has their own personality. Sliding into the melody note adds even more flavor!

Example 2 slides into the second scale degree.

EXAMPLE 2

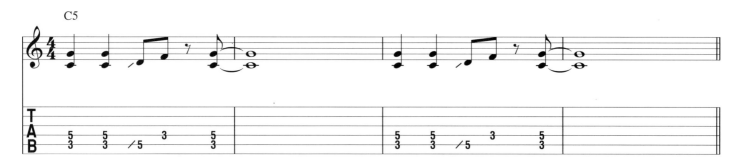

Example 3 slides into the b3rd.

EXAMPLE 3

Example 4 uses the natural 3rd.

EXAMPLE 4

Example 5 uses the natural 4th.

EXAMPLE 5

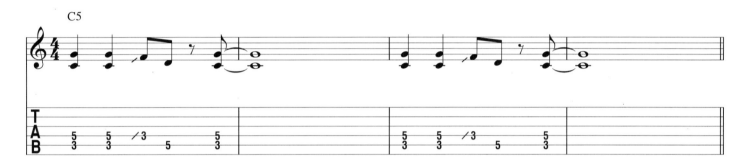

Example 6 uses the raised 5th.

EXAMPLE 6

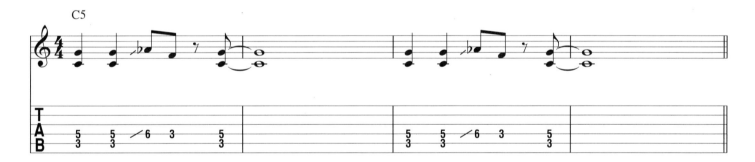

Example 7 slides into the natural 6th.

EXAMPLE 7

Example 8 uses the ♭7th and the octave note.

EXAMPLE 8

The One-Finger, Major-Minor Trick ▶

You can play every major and minor chord with *one finger*. You read that right. Have you been trying to avoid F major? Maybe you have no idea how to play G# minor? Or, do you simply want more options? This is for you!

Let's talk about major chords first. Remember that G major hiding in plain sight from the E–G–A, One-Finger Blues Trick? That beautiful harmony we get "for free" on those open strings can become an A major if we just barre with our first finger across the second, third, and fourth strings at the second fret. A precise strum with your pick produces the three notes we need for A, right? That one-finger A chord can now glide up and down the neck. C major is achieved by a barre at the fifth fret; D major is a barre at the seventh fret. And that F that was referenced earlier is up at the tenth fret. Here are the chord sequences to get you started:

EXAMPLE 1

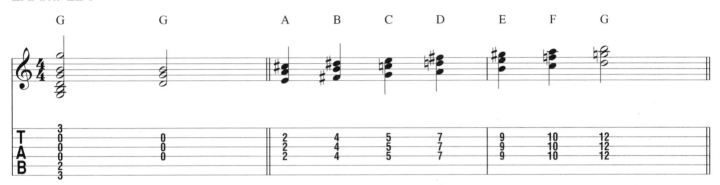

The minor chord component begins with the three open treble strings that we strum as part of the traditional E minor chord. Those three are enough to satisfy the definition of E minor. With that in mind, we can barre the three treble strings and play all sorts of minor chords. The A minor chord waits for you at the fifth fret, for example, while D minor is at the tenth fret. Get the idea? Here's the sequence:

EXAMPLE 2

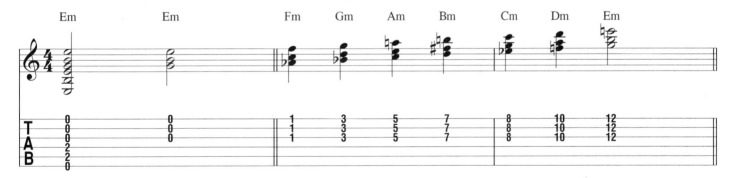

Do you see how you could play an entire song with one finger? This is a great approach when playing with someone who is already strumming the conventional chords. You're going to love how these new *voicings* bring a song to life!

Example 3 bops you through a classic major chord sequence. It's almost too easy, right?

EXAMPLE 3

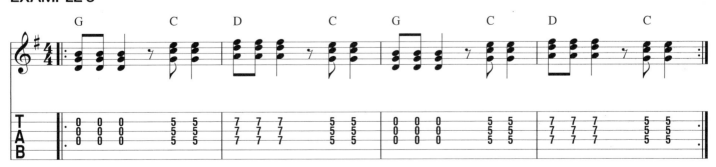

Example 4 guides you through the timeless I–vi–ii–V pop progression. Picture how great this will sound with another guitarist playing the conventional C, Am, Dm, and G chords!

EXAMPLE 4

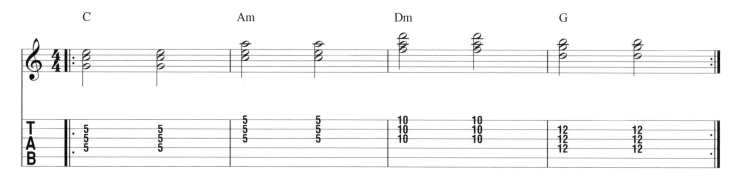

Example 5 mixes major and minor chords in the style of "The House of the Rising Sun." Voicing your chords this way can really help the guitar to fit into a mix that includes keyboard, bass, and drums.

EXAMPLE 5

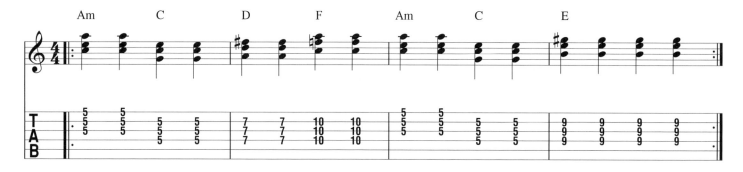

The A-D Trick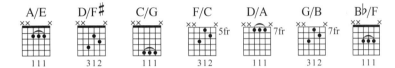

The One-Finger, Major–Minor Trick leads nicely into this next concept. You start with a one-finger A chord, using a barre at the second fret. Then, keeping the barre in place, arch over your second and third fingers to turn the A major into a D major.

Practice until you can consistently hear all three strings ringing. Some find more success on higher frets at first. Move it up the neck, and you'll be playing I–IV chord progressions all over the place! Here are the chord grids in the first example:

EXAMPLE 1

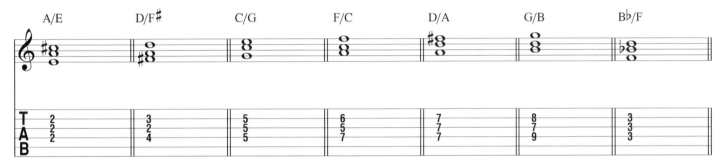

And here are the chords in standard notation and tablature:

Don't let these "slash chord" names hang you up. Just as with B/F♯, A/E translates as an A major chord with E as the lowest note.

In Example 2, get ready to play "name-that-tune"—it will probably ring a bell!

EXAMPLE 2

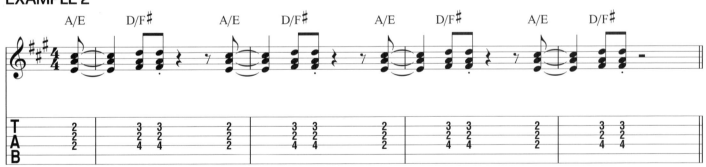

Example 3 is a little twist on Example 1, and it includes a trip up a couple frets from C to D.

EXAMPLE 3

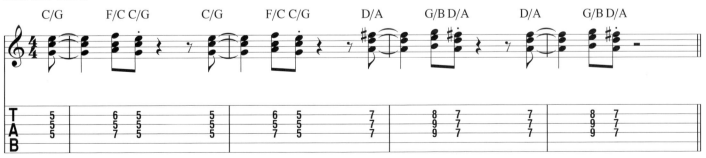

Now I hope you're sitting down because we could re-imagine the D as the I chord and the A as the V chord. Whoa! This reverse opens up more possibilities. The fun never stops, my friend!

Example 4 presents F as the I chord, with B♭ as the IV and C as the V. Sound familiar?

EXAMPLE 4

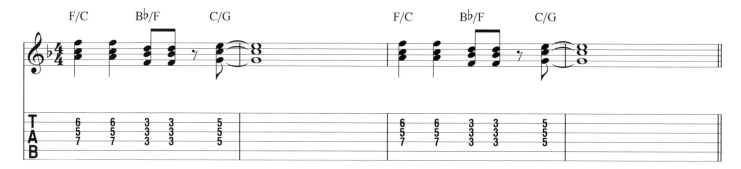

The Fmaj7 Trick

Here's one of my favorite tricks because of how gosh-darn pretty (or dissonant!) it can sound. There are many creative possibilities here.

Let's start with the elegant Fmaj7. It's easy and sophisticated and a great potential substitute for good old F major. We can strum it, of course, but arpeggiating it really brings out the sweet harmony provided by the open first string.

Fmaj7

Every time you slide the Fmaj7 "grip" up, the open first string provides a new sonic complement. There are some powerful sounds waiting for you—explore the neck and make note of the chord names for future reference. Example 1 shows you the sequence.

EXAMPLE 1

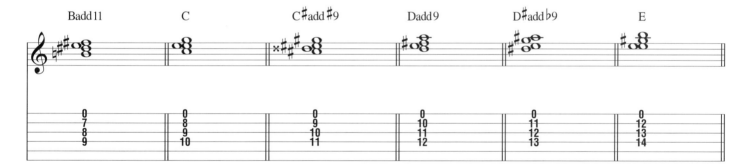

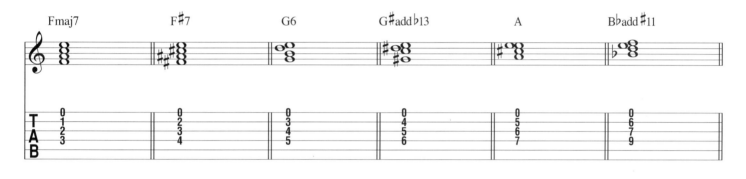

Example 2 features a pretty arpeggio that allows us to hear the open first string prominently.

EXAMPLE 2

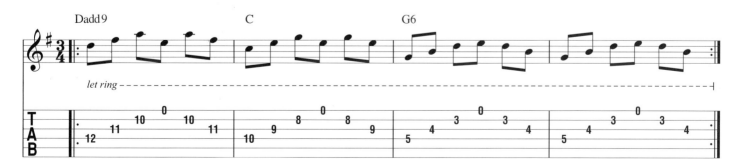

Example 3 glides up and down the neck in the key of C. You now have new options when you come across our old favorites, C, F, and G!

EXAMPLE 3

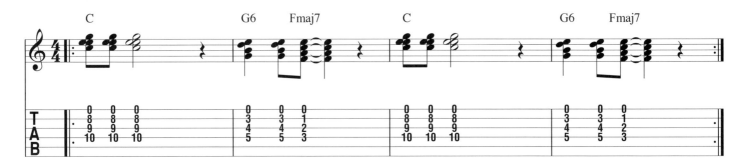

Example 4 does the same in the key of E. Let those strings ring!

EXAMPLE 4

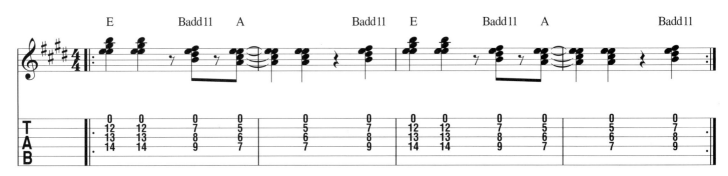

The E Major Trick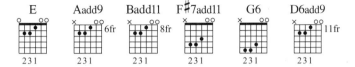

I just had to include this next related trick. It's like the Fmaj7 Trick but based on the E major chord grip. Now we have *two* open treble strings harmonizing in unique ways as our fretting hand moves up the neck. Again, make note of the chord names.

You might find musical magic pairing up one of these while a partner plays the conventional equivalent. Just because someone else is playing a "boring" chord doesn't mean you have to!

Example 1 starts with our open-position E and glides up the neck to our IV and V chords.

EXAMPLE 1

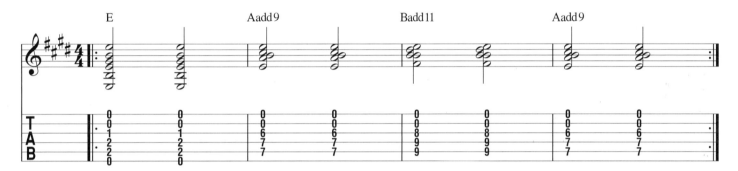

Example 2 is in the key of B. You'll arpeggiate through the beauty of the Badd11 and F#7add11 as well as the "comfort" of the E. It sounds pretty, right?

EXAMPLE 2

Example 3 presents an option for you the next time you're tasked with strumming through G, A, and D chords. When strummed this way, you'll be getting a big, "wide-open" effect.

EXAMPLE 3

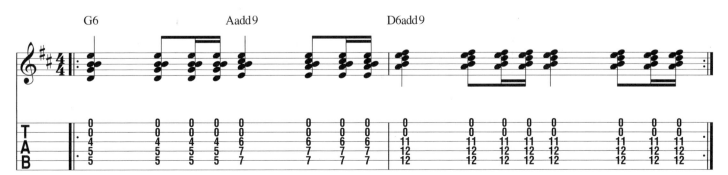

The Open-String Blues Trick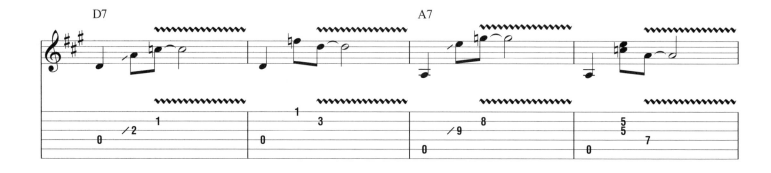

Many years ago, I watched footage of blues players playing in this style. I asked myself, "What are they doing, and why does it look so effortless?"

Relying on your open strings and letting them ring is the key here. We are in the key of A, so we can employ the open bass strings as we maneuver through a 12-bar blues progression. Use a pick or your right-hand fingers for this one!

I have some fingering tips for you: Use your first two fingers for the sliding riffs, such as in measures 1 and 2. In measure 4, I like to use my second and third fingers for the little, two-string bend—save your index for the little barre across the first two strings at the fifth fret. Then, barre again with your first finger in measure 8. Lastly, keep your tempo slow—let the guitar speak for itself! "Less-is-more" is the philosophy here!

EXAMPLE 1

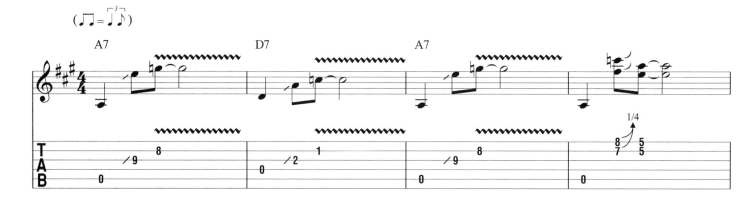

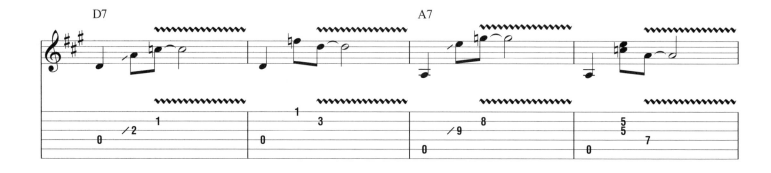

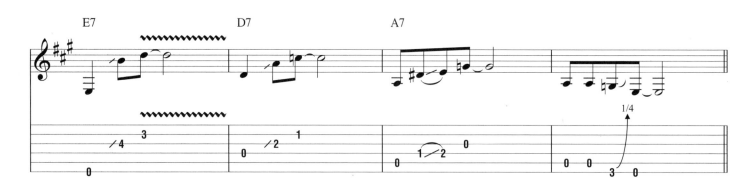

The Only Two-Chord Blues Trick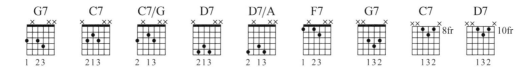

When I learned these two chord "grips," I found I could cruise through countless blues progressions! Only *two*? Yeah!

Blues rhythm guitar relies on dominant 7th chords, and these formations cover every 7th chord you'll ever need. (Dominant 7ths are four-note chords, but we are *implying* these chords here. That's how it's done!)

Here are the chord grips we'll use for the following examples:

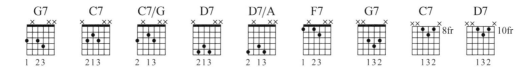

Example 1 features the chords you'll need for a blues in G. There's G7 with the root note found on the sixth string and C7 with the root note found on the fifth string. You can alter the C7 by omitting the root note (!) and anchoring the chord on the sixth string (the fifth degree of the C major scale). Both versions are great! The same goes for the D7 that rounds out the trio.

EXAMPLE 1

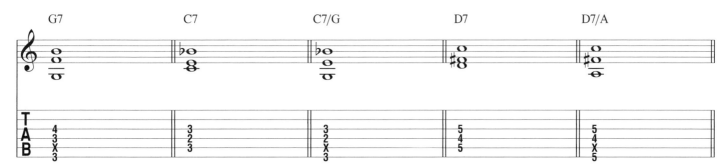

Example 2 employs these chords in a 12-bar blues in the key of G. Keep the tempo slow and work on smooth chord transitions. It's crucial to keep the third finger touching the third string *at all times*.

EXAMPLE 2

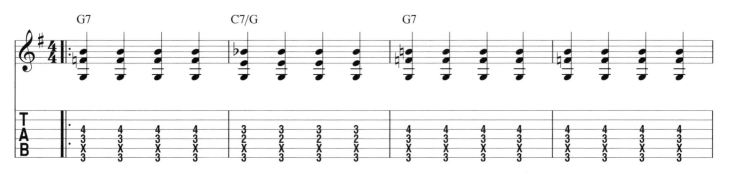

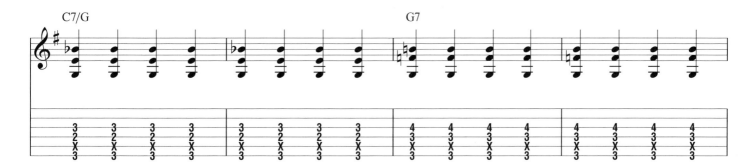

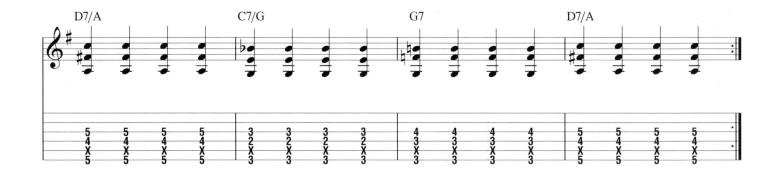

Example 3 flips the concept, putting us in the key of C, so C7 is our I chord, F7 is the IV chord, and G7 is the V chord.

EXAMPLE 3

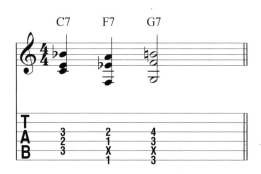

Example 4 gives you a bonus chord grip on the treble strings. This formation reminds me of a D major chord, just moved to the second, third, and fourth strings. It's so accessible! I like sliding into this one from a lower fret. The root note has been placed in parentheses so that you are aware of its location. For fun, try fretting it with your thumb!

EXAMPLE 4

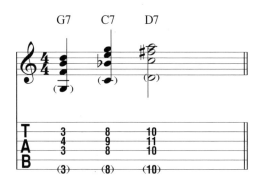

The Power Chord–Open String Trick ▶

I confess that I love including open strings whenever I can. It's like a gift waiting for us anytime we want it! Lifting off your index gives you access to some powerful sounds. Check these out!

Example 1 showcases three "families" of power chords that "play well" with open bass strings. When playing power chords, use your first and third fingers, or first and fourth if the stretch is too much.

EXAMPLE 1

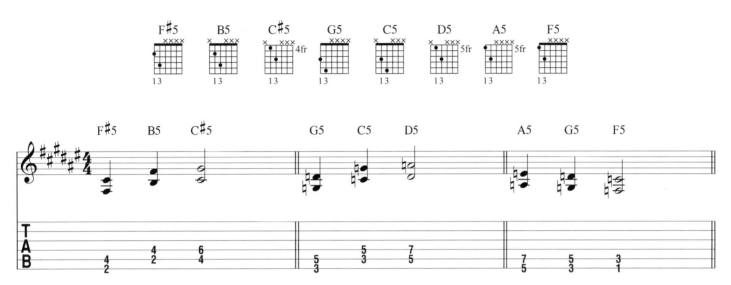

In Example 2, the open E and A strings add a nice dark touch to this riff in the key of F#. When playing the open string, lift only your first finger!

EXAMPLE 2

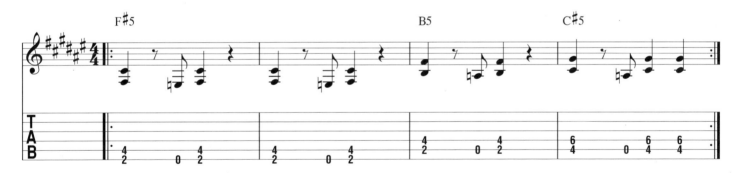

Example 3 is in the key of G, where the open E and A maintain a major-key sound, but contrast nicely with the power chords.

EXAMPLE 3

In Example 4, notice how the open E string firmly grounds this descending power chord riff.

EXAMPLE 4

The Pinky Sixth Trick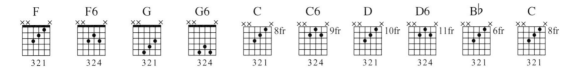

Start with an easy major chord grip and bring it to life with a simple pinky move! For me, this always brings to mind a mix of country, rockabilly, and early rock 'n' roll. And it gives your fourth finger something important to do! Here are the chords we'll use in the following examples:

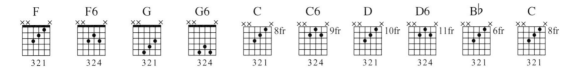

Example 1 gives you a "Maximum F" using all six strings. Don't sweat because we are "extracting" a smaller F chord played as a simple three-finger, three-note triad. Be precise with your pick to avoid strumming unwanted strings. Add the fourth finger to grab our new note (the sixth degree of the F major scale, if you're curious!) Then, repeat this to modify G, C, and D chords.

EXAMPLE 1

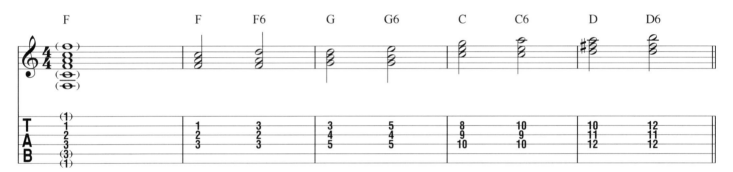

In Example 2, let's add some rhythm! Keep your first finger down at all times, even when the fourth finger "cancels it out."

EXAMPLE 2

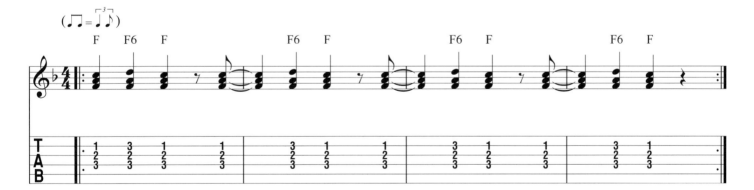

On the next page, Example 3 walks you up the neck using G, C, and D chords. This trick always sounds great! Down-up strumming gives this a smooth feel. Listen for the new note added by the fourth finger; if you can't hear it clearly, neither can your fans!

EXAMPLE 3

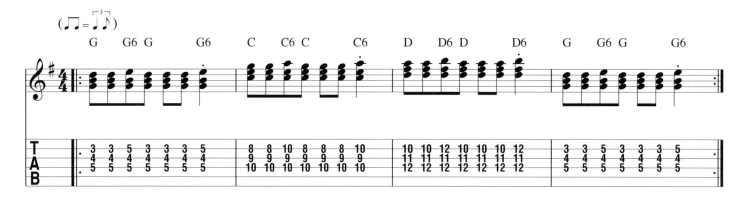

Example 4 uses an *arpeggio* approach to call attention to our new note.

EXAMPLE 4

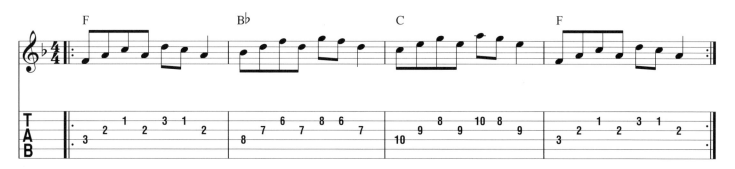

The Melodic Shuffle Trick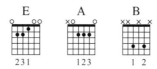

Guitarists refer to lots of patterns as "shuffles." They typically share a swinging feel, but each one has its own personality. Here's one of my favorites! Use a pick-and-finger approach, or pluck with a thumb and finger. Here are the chord grids we'll use:

In Example 1, we start with our conventional E and A major chords, but then we "reduce" them in Example 2. Do you see how the B chord is just the A moved up two frets?

EXAMPLE 1

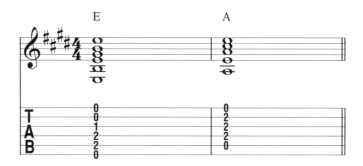

EXAMPLE 2

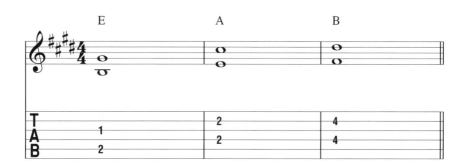

Examples 3 through 5 are the foundation. For the A and B shuffles, I recommend beginning with your second finger on the D string and the third finger on the B string.

EXAMPLE 3

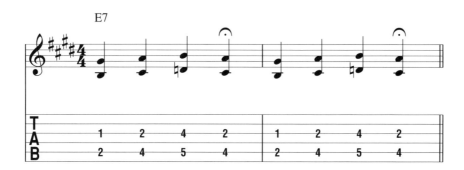

EXAMPLE 4

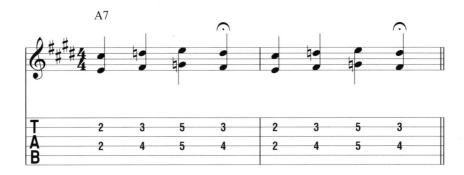

EXAMPLE 5

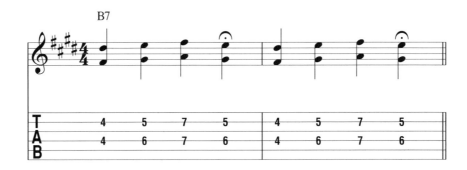

Example 6 puts everything together with open strings to fill in the gaps. It's so hip! Fortunately, this sounds great at a slow tempo, so relax and practice it patiently.

EXAMPLE 6

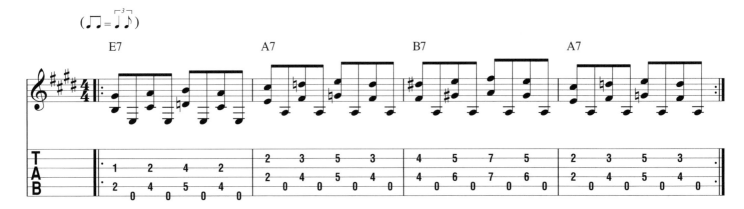

The Chord Play Trick ▶

Several years ago, I was stumped by a chord I could hear on a recording but couldn't recognize. A wiser guitarist pointed out that the mystery chord was a simple C major without the first finger, a Cmaj7. Eureka! And it was even easier than C!

I've been on a mission ever since to make sure my students are aware of this neat trick. All those open-position chords you've learned have tons of hidden potential! Here are the chords we'll use in the following examples:

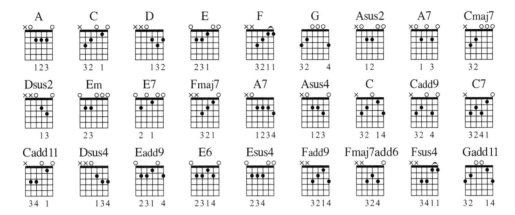

The Fmaj7add6 voicing can be a mouthful to say, but you can look at it as a variation of an F6 chord. Example 1 gets us started with our familiar major chords. (Feel free to experiment with minor chords, too.)

EXAMPLE 1

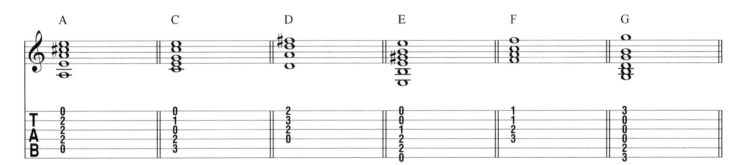

In Example 2, beautiful chords are achieved by removing a finger from your major chord.

EXAMPLE 2

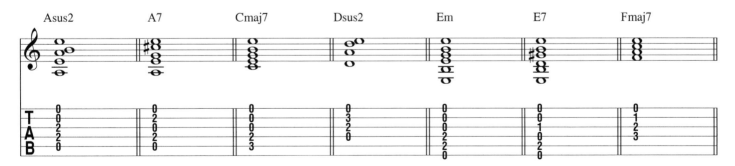

In Example 3 on the next page, these other chords are achieved by adding a finger, usually the fourth.

EXAMPLE 3

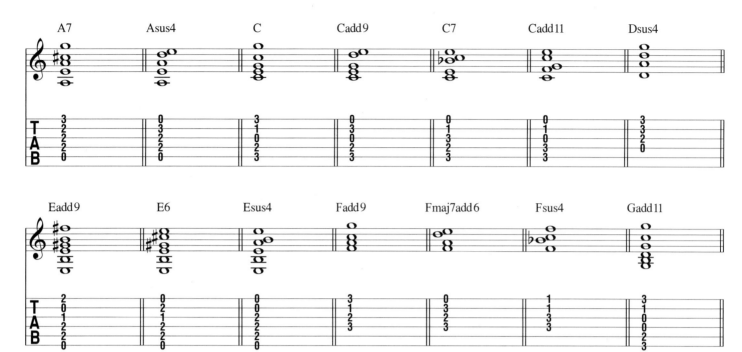

PART 3
Lead Guitar Tricks

The Double Stop Trick ▶

So much of the guitar's power comes from our ability to combine tones, as in *we can easily play two strings at once!* Let's add this trick to your skill set immediately, right here, right now. We'll use the most common rock scale (the pentatonic scale) as our framework. Playing double stops in this context will reveal some very familiar sounds!

Example 1 shows the A minor pentatonic scale.

EXAMPLE 1

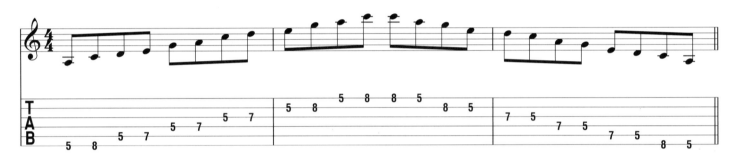

In Example 2, using this scale as a starting point, you can find the juiciest double stops! Barre these using single fingers across two strings at the same time. For starters, how about using the first finger to play the 5s, the second finger on the 7s, and the third finger on the 8s?

EXAMPLE 2

For the most control in Example 3, let your first three fingers all help with this bend. It's sweet, yet subtle!

EXAMPLE 3

Of course, you can combine single notes with double stops as shown in Examples 4 and 5. What a sound!

EXAMPLE 4

EXAMPLE 5

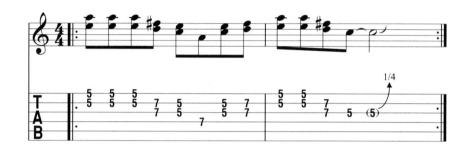

Example 6 is easier than it looks and gives you that classic "train whistle" effect!

EXAMPLE 6

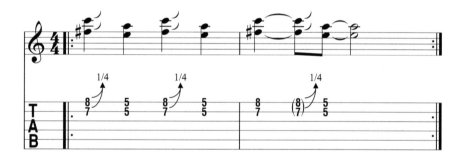

The Box 1 Trick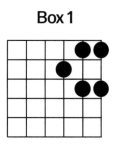

It's time to learn the cutest thing ever. That's right—*cute!* This five-note pattern is easy to play and memorize, sounds great, and travels well up and down the neck. That's why players of all stripes have always employed this humble "box" pattern. It's called a box because it looks like an odd, little square. Its technical name is the pentatonic scale. It works not only for rock, but for country, blues, and bluegrass as well—basically all popular music.

Isn't that great? Let's learn it, and then put it to use!

Box 1

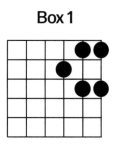

In Example 1, we "place" the box at the third, fourth, and fifth frets. Make sure you follow the recommended fingering: first finger playing the third-fret notes, second finger on the fourth-fret note, and third finger on the fifth-fret notes. Play it as written, using down-up picking. Memorize it as soon as you can!

EXAMPLE 1

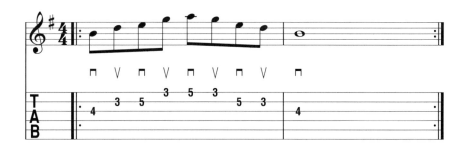

Now hang on to your hats! Box 1 is an example of a pentatonic scale, and pentatonic scales have a dual identity: major and minor.

Example 2 is a Box 1-based riff to be played over a G major chord. Note that G would be considered the "root note" in this context, so I've ended the riff there.

EXAMPLE 2

On the next page, Example 3 sounds great over an E minor chord. Again, we are ending on the root note, which is E. Isn't that great? This means that this single box pattern can be used in twice as many songs as you imagined. In this case, you can use it in songs in the key of E minor and G major. In case you're curious, this is because the five notes you've just been playing (B, D, E, G, and A) are the same notes comprising both the G major pentatonic scale and the E minor pentatonic scale.

EXAMPLE 3

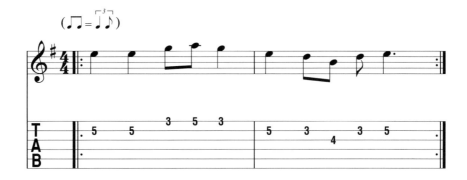

You can "decorate" this scale by sliding into notes as indicated in Examples 4 and 5. Experiment with bending the high A note to B♭ as shown in Example 6.

EXAMPLE 4

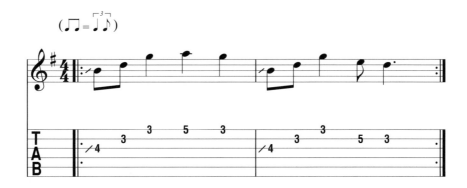

EXAMPLE 5

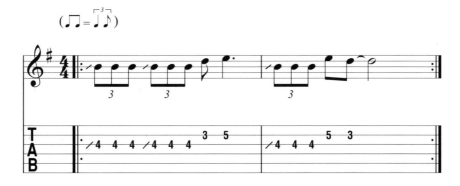

EXAMPLE 6

The internet is full of backing tracks in every key. Improvise with Box 1 over these backing tracks to truly develop your lead guitar skills!

The Box 1-Box 2 Trick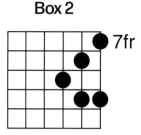

We all want to be that player who zips up and down the neck as they improvise. Did you know there's a *trick* to it? It's done by connecting the dots! We're about to connect Box 1 up the neck with the very similar Box 2.

In the diagrams below, you can see how Box 2 looks almost the same as Box 1. (Note that we are placing it at the seventh through tenth frets.) If we named each note, we see the same five pitches again: E, G, A, B, and D.

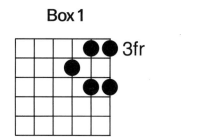

Practice Example 1 several times—note how Box 2 is almost the same pattern as Box 1!

EXAMPLE 1

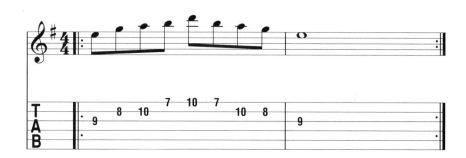

I've found the key to connecting Box 1 with Box 2 is gliding my second finger quickly from the fourth fret to the ninth, as shown in Example 2. This way, I'm instantly ready to play my new box!

EXAMPLE 2

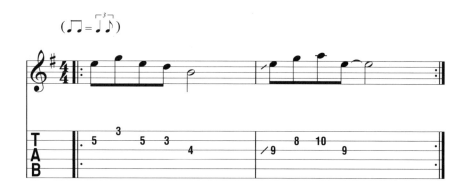

In Example 3 on the next page, we reverse the pattern to get back to Box 1.

EXAMPLE 3

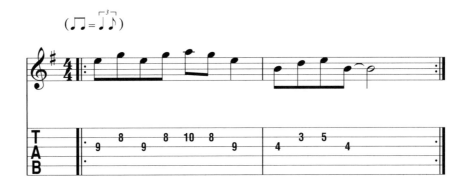

In Example 4, we change the key just to make sure that you get the principle here.

EXAMPLE 4

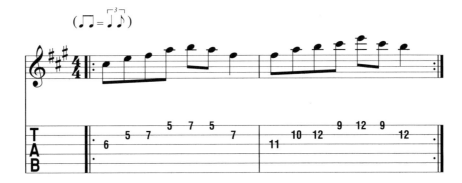

What if Box 1 is so high up the neck that you run out of accessible frets before you can reach Box 2, as with many acoustic guitars? Aha!—Box 2 is also waiting back down the neck, one octave lower, as found in Example 5.

EXAMPLE 5

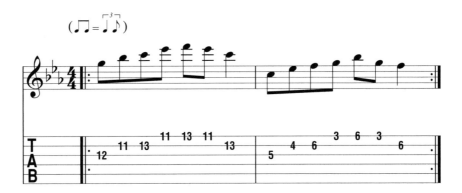

The Sixth Trick

Sixths are just about the prettiest sound on the guitar! And you can easily add them to your bag of tricks so that you can use them for melodies, intros, riffs, and soloing.

In Example 1, we have the first three notes of a C major scale.

EXAMPLE 1

For Example 2, let's harmonize those notes by fretting part of a C major chord. Fret with your first two fingers to start, then keep your second finger fretting the D string and use your third finger on the B string. Use your pick and middle finger to "pinch" both strings simultaneously, or just use your bare thumb and any finger.

EXAMPLE 2

In Example 3, we can move this trick higher up the neck or over to the first and third strings, as shown in Example 4.

EXAMPLE 3

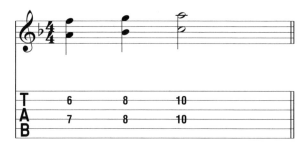

EXAMPLE 4

Let's reverse it in Example 5!

EXAMPLE 5

Experiment with sliding into these notes, too! Example 6 shows you how.

EXAMPLE 6

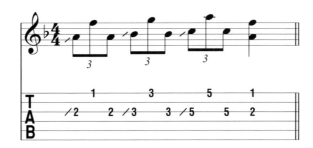

Let's not stop with major chords! Examples 7 and 8 apply this approach to E minor and A minor chords, respectively.

EXAMPLE 7

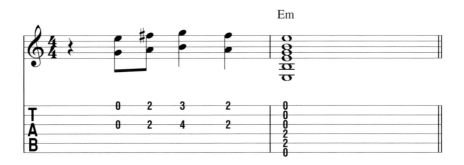

EXAMPLE 8

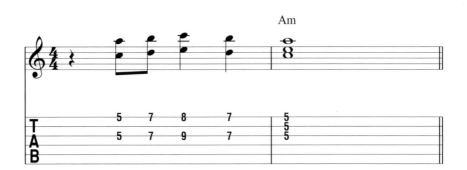

The Turnaround-Intro Trick

One of the most convenient blues guitar tricks I ever learned was using a turnaround as an intro. *Duh!* What better way to lead the band into the starting I chord than the same turnaround that you were going to use at the end of the 12-bar sequence? And every tune benefits from an intro, if only to get the attention of the drummer!

Example 1 is perhaps the most famous turnaround of them all, so make sure you have it handy as an intro. Here it is in the key of E. I like using my second finger on the G string and my third finger on the E. Be sure to really lean into the sweet hammer-on on the G string.

EXAMPLE 1

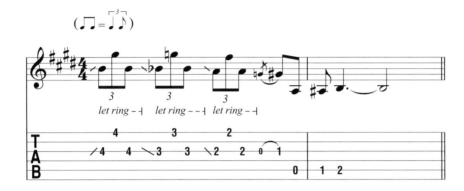

In the following examples, use a pick-and-finger approach to "pinch" the strings.

Example 2 is one for a blues in the key of A based on the open-position A7 chord.

EXAMPLE 2

Example 3 is in the key of G, but notice the familiar E7 formation using your first two fingers.

EXAMPLE 3

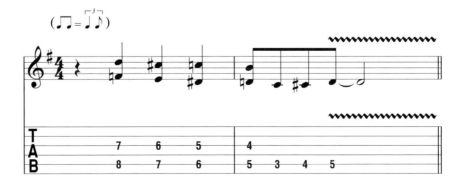

Example 4 is in the key of C. Plant your fourth finger on the first string, and get ready to *s–t–r–e–t–c–h*!

EXAMPLE 4

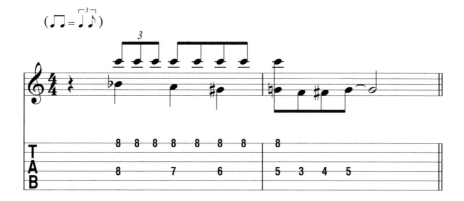

The Dorian Mode Trick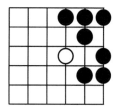

Faced with soloing over a minor key song, you might reach automatically for a pentatonic scale. Instead, reach into your trick bag for the Dorian mode. The results are dark and rich, and your band members will stand in awe. (Results may vary.) A *mode* is just a major scale viewed from a different perspective. Scared? Don't be. Let's check it out!

The diagram below shows a major scale shape with the Dorian root shown as an open circle.

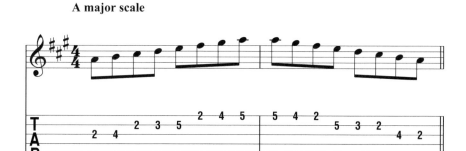

Example 1 gives you an easy way to play an A major scale. It starts on one A and ends an octave higher on the next A. In this context, we call A the "root note."

EXAMPLE 1

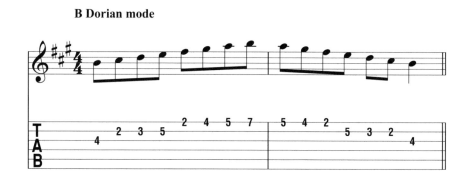

In Example 2, let's omit the first A and start on the second note (B). Then, we'll add on a B at the end. This is the B Dorian mode, and now B is the "root note." You just played an A major scale starting on the second degree. That's the Dorian mode in a nutshell.

EXAMPLE 2

Of course, you can still reach back for that first A you played in Example 1. Any note from the A major scale is fair game. But because our hypothetical song is in the key of B minor, you'll find the most musical satisfaction when you return to any B note.

Now you're ready to find some songs and backing tracks in the key of B minor and begin soloing along with them, using your B Dorian mode.

Example 3 shows you a B Dorian riff.

EXAMPLE 3

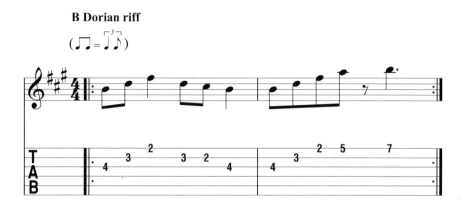

Example 4 is a C major scale with a "built-in" D Dorian mode. This is great for songs in D minor.

EXAMPLE 4

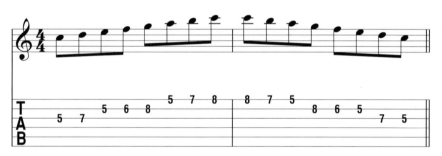

Example 5 is a D major scale, AKA the E Dorian mode. Get the idea?

EXAMPLE 5

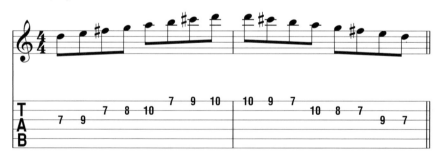

Here's the bottom line: If you know the song is in a minor key, find out which key and mentally go back a whole step. Are you playing a minor blues in G? All you have to do is think back a whole step from G to F. Next, locate your F major scale. Begin to improvise using the F major scale with the knowledge that the second note of the F scale (G) is your "home" as you jam out. Get it?

The Mixolydian Mode Trick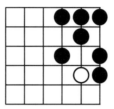

The Mixolydian mode is another one that's very useful. The "trick" here has the same result as the Dorian mode— creative sounds beyond the ubiquitous pentatonic scales.

Again, we use a major scale as our starting point. However, instead of making the second note our root, here we focus on the fifth note. Just be reminded that it's still a major scale. The result is a sweet, happy collection of notes that swing neatly when improvising over a major-key blues tune.

The diagram below shows a major scale shape with the Mixolydian root shown as an open circle.

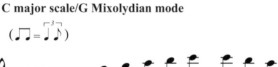

Example 1 comes from the C major scale/G Mixolydian mode. Note that the fifth note or degree of the C major scale is G. Five is the magic number here.

EXAMPLE 1

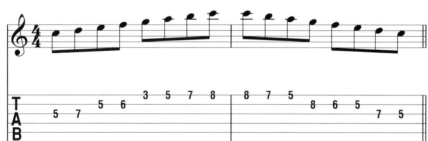

Example 2 is a riff that dances around the C scale, but because it begins and ends on G, it takes on the identity of the G Mixolydian mode. (Imagine an up-tempo, 12-bar blues in G, hopping and bopping along in the background.)

EXAMPLE 2

Want to blow a bit over a blues in another key? How about the key of A? You'll need to know which scale has A as the fifth degree. (It's D major.) Or, find an A note and go backwards seven frets (D again). That's the major scale you'll employ to solo!

Let's get started with the D major scale/A Mixolydian mode in Example 3. It shows you this concept through a scale played in swung eighth notes.

EXAMPLE 3

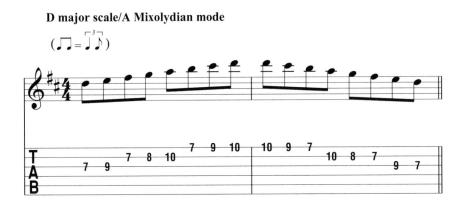

Example 4 is a peppy A Mixolydian phrase. The notes are from a D major scale, but the phrase is composed around the A note. Move over, pentatonic scales!

EXAMPLE 4

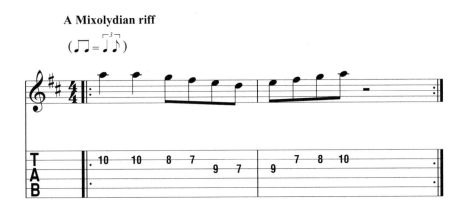